LETTiNG GO!

AN ACTiViTY BOOK FOR YOUNG PEOPLE WHO NEED SUPPORT THROUGH EXPERiENCES OF LOSS, CHANGE, DiSAPPOiNTMENT, AND GRiEF

Kane Miller
A DIVISION OF EDC PUBLISHING

First American Edition 2020
Kane Miller, A Division of EDC Publishing

© 2020 Studio Press
Written by Dr. Sharie Coombes, Child, Family & Adult Psychotherapist,
Ed.D, MA (PsychPsych), DHypPsych(UK), Senior QHP, B.Ed.
Illustrated by Ellie O'Shea
Designed by Rob Ward
Edited by Frankie Jones

First published in the UK in 2020 by Studio Press,
an imprint of Bonnier Books UK

For information contact:
Kane Miller, A Division of EDC Publishing
PO Box 470663
Tulsa, OK 74147-0663
www.kanemiller.com
www.edcpub.com
www.usbornebooksandmore.com

Library of Congress Control Number: 2019952416

Printed in China
3 5 7 9 10 8 6 4

ISBN: 978-1-68464-124-6

LETTING GO!

THIS BOOK BELONGS TO

_____

WELCOME TO LETTING GO!

Author
DR. SHARIE COOMBES
Child and Family Psychotherapist

Sometimes in life, we have to get used to changes we wouldn't have chosen for ourselves. This activity book is a great way to get you thinking, talking, and working through the things that are troubling you, so you can get on with being you, enjoying life, and letting go.

The activities will help you to understand and soothe your feelings, feel more comfortable, improve your confidence about the future, and talk to others about your hurt and worries (if you want to). You could use this book in a quiet, cozy place where you can think and feel relaxed, and it's up to you which pages you do. You might do a page a day, or complete lots of pages at once. You can start anywhere in the book and even come back to a page many times. There are no rules!

Sometimes we can feel so stuck that we believe nothing will help, but there is always a solution to every problem. Nothing is so big it can't be sorted out or talked about, even if it feels that way. You could show some of these activities to important people in your life to help you explain how you are feeling and to get help with what is upsetting you. You can talk to an adult you trust at school, or ask an adult at home to take you to the doctor for more support.

Lots of children need a bit of extra help every now and then, and here are three organizations you can turn to if you don't want to talk to people you know. They have helped thousands of children with every kind of problem and will know how to help you. They won't be shocked by anything you tell them, however bad it seems to you.

CHILDHELP

Childhelp is dedicated to looking after children. Their free, confidential help line puts you in touch with a counselor any time, day or night.

Tel: 1-800-422-4453
www.childhelp.org

CRISIS TEXT LINE

Crisis Text Line serves anyone, in any time of crisis, by providing access to free, 24/7 support and information via text message from a trained crisis counselor.

Text HOME to 741741
(Text lines are open 24/7. There is no charge if your cell phone plan is with AT&T, T-Mobile, Sprint, or Verizon. For other carriers, standard text message rates apply.)
www.crisistextline.org

YOUR LIFE YOUR VOICE

Offers universal crisis portals for children/youth by phone, text, and online, to reach qualified professional crisis counselors.

Tel: 1-800-448-3000 (24 hours)
www.yourlifeyourvoice.org
Text VOICE to 20121 to start a text conversation, open every day, 11 AM to 1 AM CST.

LETTING GO

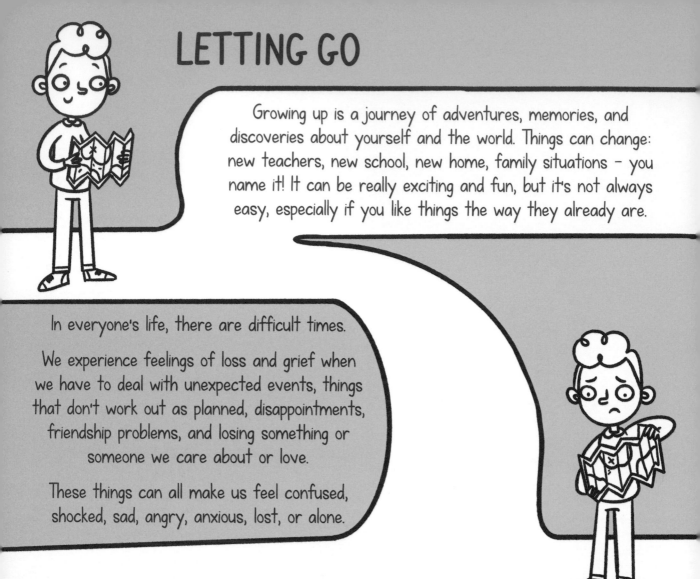

Growing up is a journey of adventures, memories, and discoveries about yourself and the world. Things can change: new teachers, new school, new home, family situations – you name it! It can be really exciting and fun, but it's not always easy, especially if you like things the way they already are.

In everyone's life, there are difficult times.

We experience feelings of loss and grief when we have to deal with unexpected events, things that don't work out as planned, disappointments, friendship problems, and losing something or someone we care about or love.

These things can all make us feel confused, shocked, sad, angry, anxious, lost, or alone.

You might not know what to think, say, or do. You might worry more, or doubt whether you'll ever feel happy again. It's normal to stop noticing all the good things around you for a while. Hang on – you'll feel better and move forward again.

Your body experiences a range of feelings every day as a result of the emotions that are made in your brain because of what it sees, feels, thinks, and believes.

You'll need time, space, and help to grieve, and to come to terms with what has happened and carry on. That's what LETTING GO is. This book was written to give you lots of ideas about how to do that and feel better. The uplifting activities show you how to notice the good things all around you, teach you coping skills, and get you back on track.

THIS IS FLO —
go with Flo and she'll help your amazing brain with LETTING GO.

LOOK FOR HER THROUGHOUT THE BOOK.

LETTING GO gets you moving forward and loving life again. It's a wonderful world out there – let's explore it together and get your sunshine back. You've got this!

GET SET...
GO WITH FLO!

TREE-MENDOUS YOU!

Like a beautiful, unique, and enchanting tree, you are made up of important parts.

JOYFUL   TIRED   SURPRISED   SAD   DELIGHTED

GUILTY

FRIENDS

BOOKS

FAMILY

PETS

MUSIC

HOBBIES

Trees have branches which grow in all directions.

Some are stronger than others, just like your feelings.

Write any feelings you've had in the last few weeks between the branches.

You have deep roots that help you grow, keeping you safe, strong, secure, and supported.

Draw YOUR roots and write what and who they are.

Many trees grow green leaves in the spring, which soak up sun and rain all summer, making energy to help the tree get bigger and stronger.

In the fall, leaves change color and drop to the ground, and the branches stay empty until the next spring. Fallen leaves break down in the soil over the cold winter, feeding the roots to keep the tree growing.

TEACHERS

FRIENDS

FAMILY

SOCCER CLEATS

PETS

HOLIDAYS

TOYS

Fill these fall leaves with things that were once part of your life but have now gone.

All these things make you who you are now. Nothing is wasted.

Color your leaves with yellows, golds, oranges, reds, purples, and browns.

Spend a moment thinking about each leaf that's fallen from your tree, and say thank you for the energy and strength it has given you. Now you're ready to let it go.

Watch it blow away on the wind.

Come back to these pages as often as you like to add roots, branches, and leaves.

I AM

Draw your face in the middle of this flower.

Ask people you care about to describe your special qualities.

Write their words on the petals.

GENTLE

SMART

KIND

HELPFUL

THOUGHTFUL

Come back to this page whenever you need to remind yourself how incredible you are.

I, I, I!

Like everyone else, you need time to think about and understand yourself so you can ask for what you need when you're LETTING GO.

When I'm upset, I ___feel sad.___
I need ___a hug.___

When I'm happy, I _____
I need _____

When I'm bored, I _____
I need _____

When I'm cross, I _____
I need _____

When I'm _____, I _____
I need _____

When I'm _____, I _____
I need _____

I'LL BE THERE

Think of all the people you can ask when you need a helping hand.

Write their names on the fingers of this helping hand to remind you.

Fill the rest of the hand with things you might need to ask for, and decorate it however you like.

Ask for a hug, some time to talk, or whatever you need from these people when you're feeling under the weather.

HAND IT OVER

Sometimes, things are just too big for us to deal with by ourselves.

What is feeling too big for you right now?

What are the most important parts of this problem?

Hand it over to someone who can help. You'll be glad you did.

Write here who you handed it over to, what happened after you did, and how it helped.

If you don't need this activity right now, save it for when you do.

Make sure you tell your friends they can **HAND IT OVER** too, if they have something troubling them.

FRIENDS WHATEVER THE WEATHER

Some friends make us feel warm, even when it rains.

Draw in any details you like, and color this picture. Write any of the things you're dealing with at the moment in the raindrops, if you want.

Or just color them in – it's up to you!

MISSING MATTERS

Your feelings matter. It's important to give them attention. When you recognize them, you'll find it easier to manage them and start **LETTING GO**.

Write or draw something or someone you miss.

What was so special about it or them?

How did it or they help you?

Fill this frame with all the things you think of when you remember it or them.

You could use words, pictures, poems, stories, memories, or anything you want.

SUNSHINE ON A RAINY DAY

Have you ever seen what happens when rain suddenly falls on a sunny day?

Or, even better, when there's a burst of sunshine on a rainy day?

Rain breaks up the sunlight into different colors so you can see them all clearly, even when you'd forgotten they were always there.

You don't get rainbows to enjoy unless there's rain. The next time you're feeling upset or hurt, and you have tears in your eyes, why not remember all the things you have in your life to enjoy right now, or to look forward to in the future?

Fill this rainbow with all those things to remind yourself of the good in your life, and keep the sunshine in your heart, even when you can't see it.

Maybe you can add your hopes and dreams and things about yourself that you are proud of.

Can you remember the colors of the rainbow?

THREE THINGS

Feeling uncomfortable, upset, or overwhelmed?

You can do this activity anywhere, anytime.

Pay attention to your breathing.

Perhaps take yourself somewhere peaceful and sit calmly. Find a quiet spot outside if you like.

Imagine you are breathing in calm and breathing out hurt, like your pain or upset.

You are part of nature.

Breathe in calm, breathe out hurt.

3:5 BREATHING

Breathe in for a count of three, and out for a count of five. Keep this going for a few minutes until you start to feel relaxed.

You're LETTING GO of what's hurting you.

While you are breathing like this, draw, write, or think about:

THREE THINGS YOU HEAR	THREE THINGS YOU SEE	THREE THINGS YOU FEEL

Why not try triangle breathing too?

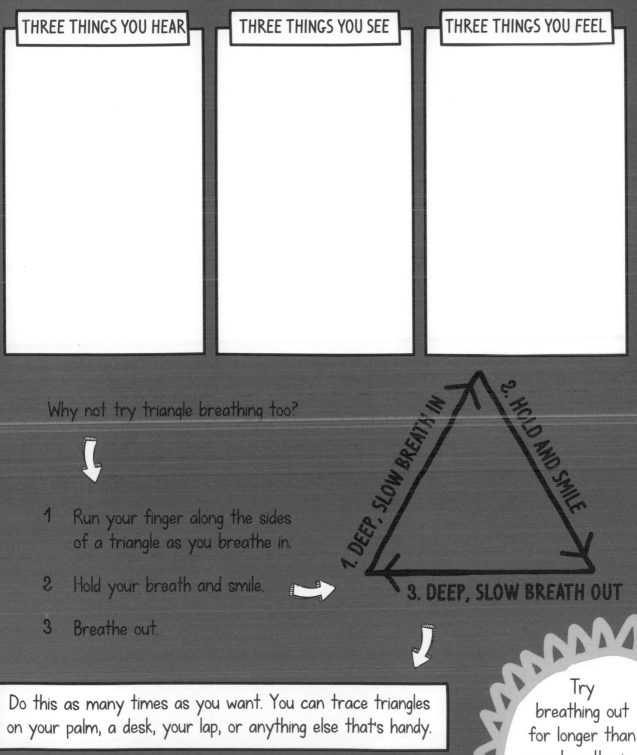

1 Run your finger along the sides
   of a triangle as you breathe in.

2 Hold your breath and smile.

3 Breathe out.

1. DEEP, SLOW BREATH IN
2. HOLD AND SMILE
3. DEEP, SLOW BREATH OUT

Do this as many times as you want. You can trace triangles
on your palm, a desk, your lap, or anything else that's handy.

Try breathing out for longer than you breathe in.

TEARS OF JOY

Turn your hurt and upset tears into tears of joy.

Fill these tears with all the things that make you laugh, feel happy, or excited.

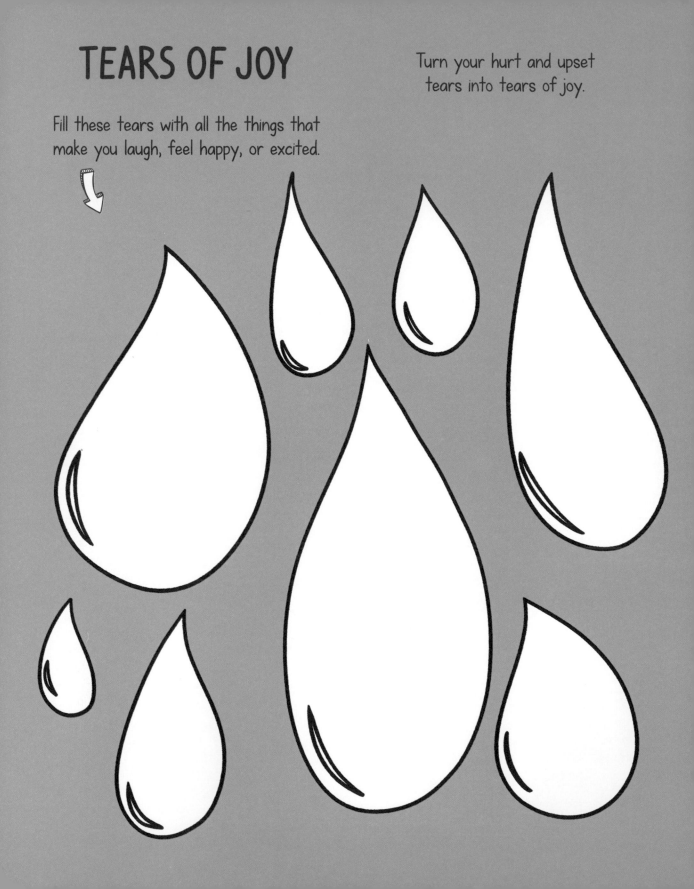

HUG FOR HAPPINESS

A hug is a wonderful way to get back to feeling happy.

It can make your tummy feel warm and your heart feel loved.

Try this activity and write down how the hug makes you feel.

Ask someone you trust for a hug right now.

Notice how it feels in your tummy and your heart.

If you can't hug someone you'd like to, close your eyes and imagine the hug - you'll still get those lovely feelings.

WHIZZ, BANG, FIZZ

Fireworks whizz high in the dark night sky, making beautiful patterns and creating new memories.

Write some thoughts, feelings, or old memories in these fireworks so you can let go of them with a bang.

Never play with fireworks – only an adult should light them.

Draw more fiery patterns in the sky and color them in, if you want.

SING SOMETHING SILLY

Now, just sing the words in whatever order you like. See what happens. Any tune you know will do – or make up your own.

Write 20 random words you hear, think, see, or remember in these weather symbols.

Add extra words as you go along if that suits you.

Sing out loud and proud! Why not challenge your family or friends to do the same thing and have a sing off?

COLOR THIS IN

THIS WILL PASS

The sun is still shining behind these rain clouds. When you start to feel it again in your heart, color the sun in however you like.

SUN DANCE

Dancing helps people to feel better, and moving makes our minds recover from upset and hurt more quickly.

When you feel down, or like clouds and rain are everywhere, grab a friend, play some music, and dance like you are trying to make your own sunshine and you're shining brightly again.

Go on – sing along and move your body every which way you can.

Keep dancing – here comes the sun!

SKIN DEEP

Find a friend or adult you feel close to who wants to do this activity with you.

Ask an adult for some hand lotion with a great smell.

YOU WILL NEED:

• Lovely smelling hand lotion

• A friendly human

• 10 minutes

Smell the lotion together, saying what it reminds you of, why you like it, and anything else you notice about it.

Decide who will go first, and spend five minutes massaging the lotion all over the other person's hands, making sure to gently cover every part and to take notice of any hurts, like bitten nails, or grazes, or other things like that.

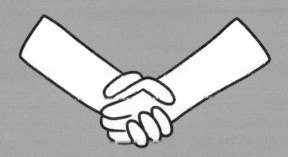

After five minutes, swap.

Ask an adult to make sure the lotion is safe for you to use.

Do this activity as often as you like, with lots of people, or always the same person – it's up to you.

INVISIBLE STRING

Even when you are by yourself, there are still people in the world who love you. You are not alone!

Your heart is joined to the hearts of everyone you love, and everyone who loves you, by an invisible string.

You always carry their love in your heart wherever you are, and whatever you are doing.

If someone is no longer alive, they still count because your hearts were connected.

WRITE YOUR NAME IN THIS HEART

IN THESE HEARTS, WRITE THE NAMES OF EVERYONE YOU'RE JOINED TO BY THE INVISIBLE STRING, AND CONNECT THE STRING TO THE HEART WITH YOUR NAME

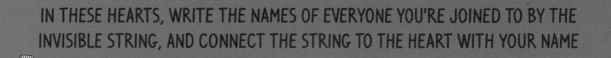

Add more hearts if you like. If your connected hearts are in different parts of the world, you could draw the strings on Flo to show how far your love travels.

WINTER WONDERLAND

In winter, the world can look cold and empty.

You can't see what used to be there, and it's easy to lose hope that it will ever be warm and green again.

Complete and color this picture, thinking all the time about what wonderful things might be underneath, ready to flourish in the springtime.

Winter is a time of rest, when nature is preparing itself for spring and is full of its own beauty.

Don't forget to appreciate what is here right now.

The world keeps turning, you keep growing, and the future is on the way.

OUT OF THE BLUE

Ever had bad news? Or something that didn't work out for you? It can feel like a storm in your mind.

Color these words and see how the storm starts and finishes – and what happens in between!

SHOCK

CONFUSED

NUMB

LETTING GO

COMFORTABLE

No one finds it easy to cope with these stormy feelings.

You'll deal with them in your own way and notice some parts of the storm more strongly than others.

ANGRY

After the shock, the feelings get jumbled up, and you'll keep whirling around them for a bit.

We learn to let go of the bad feelings and keep our lovely memories.

UPSET

The next time you're swept up in this feelings storm, you'll understand what is happening.

Why not explain it to someone else who is going through their own storm, too?

CALMER

FIZZBUMBLES

While you are **LETTING GO**, don't get in a boiling buzz. Make up your own feeling words, and turn any angry, fizzy, or fed up feelings into funny ones.

FIZZBUMBLES

BUZZYGRUMP

BEE-NOYED

See if you can slip these words into a conversation with someone else – your word might make it into the dictionary one day!

MAGICAL MIRACLE

If you had a magical unicorn and you could ask it to perform a miracle right now, what one thing would you change?

What is better now that you've changed it?

Who will benefit?

How?

Who else will notice that this has changed?

GOT THE BLUES

Color these mandalas in shades of greens, blues, and purples – my favorite colors!

LET IT GO JAR

A thought or a feeling isn't a fact. You don't have to listen to it.

Make a special jar where you can put all the things you need to let go of as they pop up.

Find a clean, empty jar with a lid.

Make a label for it.

Decorate it with drawings or stickers.

Keep it in a closet or drawer.

Whenever you have a thought you'd like to let go of, write it down on a slip of paper or a sticky note, fold it up, and trap it in this jar without air or light. It's a good activity to do first thing in the morning and at bedtime.

When your jar's full, add water and leave it for a few hours.

Drain it through a sieve or colander.

Squeeze and mush up the paper, then flatten it into a circle, square, or any other shape you like.

When it's dry, use it to write a note to someone you'd like to thank for helping you.

Lay it between two sheets of paper towel and leave it to dry.

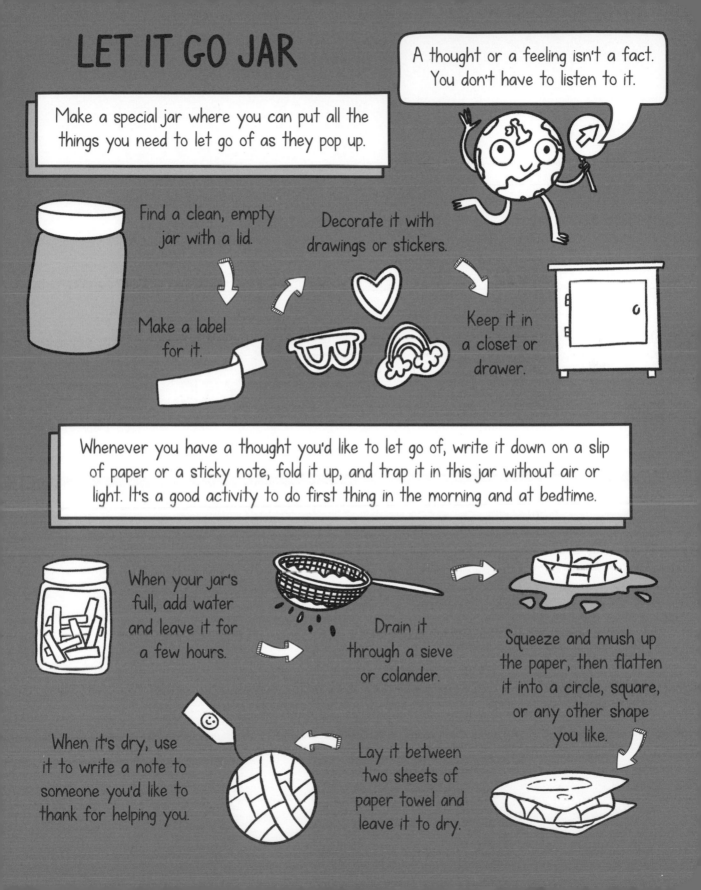

HEART HEALER

Being in nature slows down your heart rate and is really good for your mind and body.

When you do this activity, your heart will thank you for taking good care of it.

Go outside and look down. Find a living, growing, or moving natural thing like an insect, a flower, a blade of grass, or whatever you like.

Don't catch it or pick it – respect its right to be free and alive.

Check your pulse and notice how fast it's going.

Take the first two fingers of your hand and place them gently on your throat, just off to one side.

If you can't feel the rhythm of your pulse, try the other side.

Count how many times it beats in a minute. This is your heart rate.

Sit or lay down and focus on watching your natural thing for one or two minutes (or longer if you like).

Don't do anything except notice the thing you are looking at.

Check your pulse again, and see if you've slowed it down.

This time, look up and find another living, growing, or moving natural thing like clouds, birds, treetops – you choose.

Repeat the activity.

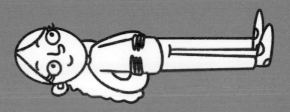

Check your pulse again right at the end, and see if you've slowed it down further.

When you've finished, notice the way you're feeling and describe it here:

MAKE YOUR HEART

Ask an adult to help you with this heart-making activity.

Look to see what you can reuse.

1 Gather your items together.

2 Cut out the heart template.

3 Pin the template to your pillowcase or folded fabric.

4 Cut around the template – make sure you now have two sides of fabric.

YOU WILL NEED:

- Fabric glue, or needle and thread and pins
- Hot glue (if needed)
- Your choice of sequins, buttons, feathers, beads, ribbons, string, yarn, leaves, seeds, dried flowers
- Fabric pens, or felt-tip pens and hair spray
- Old pillowcase, or some plain fabric folded in two
- Favorite scent
- Stuffing – you could use toy filling from a craft store or you could cut up old or spare socks or fabric scraps (make sure they're clean!)
- Piece of ribbon, string, or yarn to put your heart on a hook or door handle
- This template
- Scissors

5 Take one heart and decorate it however you like, with your choice of items. You could write messages or favorite names or words on the fabric. If you use normal felt-tip pens, spray hair spray over it to set it.

6 Sew or glue the two pieces together, leaving one side open for filling your heart.

7 Fill your heart with your chosen stuffing.

8 Glue or sew up the opening.

9 Glue or sew on your ribbon and display your beautiful heart for everyone to see. Spray scent on it if you like.

Make sure to ask an
adult for help when using
scissors, needles, and pins.

You could write a note to
put inside your heart about
something you wish for or love.

Sew along the
dashed line.

THEY THINK IT'S ALL OVER!

Just when the caterpillar thought everything was over, it began to fly!

Think of a few memories of when you felt like this caterpillar, but something good came along and changed everything for you.

Don't worry if you can't remember them all – keep coming back every time you think of one and draw or write your thoughts on the leaves.

TREE RINGS

Whatever their shape or size, we have to come to terms with loss, unwelcome changes, and disappointments. You can do it!

Ask an adult to do this activity with you.

Loss, unwelcome changes, and disappointments happen in our lives. Some are little things that only affect us for a short while, and others have a big impact for some time. It's very normal to find it hard to understand what's going on.

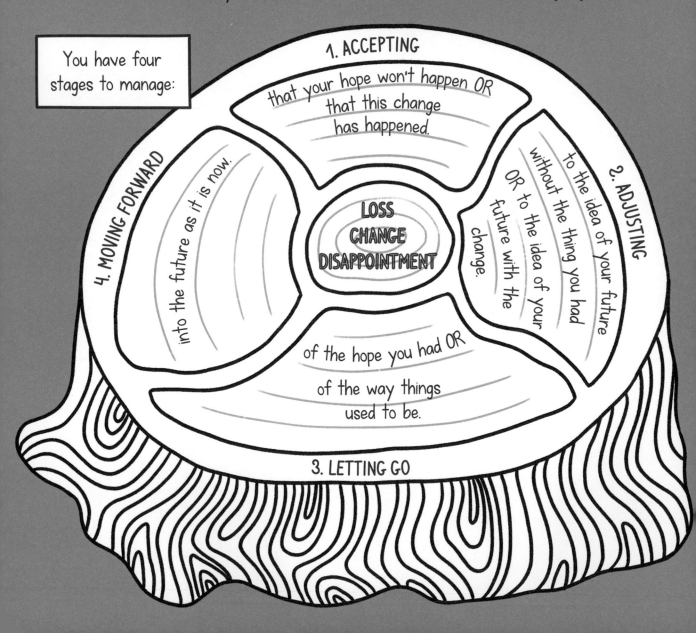

You have four stages to manage:

1. ACCEPTING that your hope won't happen OR that this change has happened.

2. ADJUSTING to the idea of your future without the thing you had OR to the idea of your future with the change.

3. LETTING GO of the hope you had OR of the way things used to be.

4. MOVING FORWARD into the future as it is now.

LOSS
CHANGE
DISAPPOINTMENT

Think of something that has been difficult for you to come to terms with recently.

Write what the difficulty was in the center of the tree rings.

Finish the sentences inside the tree.

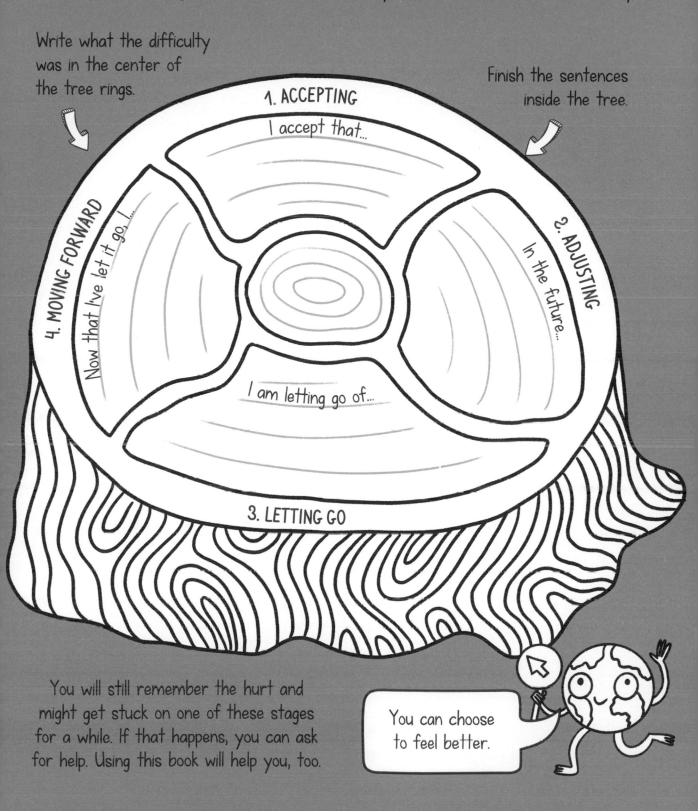

1. ACCEPTING

I accept that...

2. ADJUSTING

In the future...

4. MOVING FORWARD

Now that I've let it go, I...

I am letting go of...

3. LETTING GO

You will still remember the hurt and might get stuck on one of these stages for a while. If that happens, you can ask for help. Using this book will help you, too.

You can choose to feel better.

WHAT'S IN MY HEART

You are a puzzle of memories, hopes, dreams, wishes, and goals.

Add the memories, hopes, dreams, and goals that you feel are the most important to you right now.

Why not ask a friend or adult to guess what's in your heart? Then see if they were right.

Ask a friend or adult to fill in their heart,
and see if you can guess any pieces correctly.

Then see if you were right.

BLUE PLANET

In this ancient forest, everything is green. You can't see what is growing out of sight underneath the surface, but when the time is right, the whole forest floor will be filled with bluebells. It will look like there is a purple-blue carpet as far as the eye can see.

Now's your time to transform your forest – cover the ground with flowers or create a purple-blue haze with crayons or pens.

This natural miracle happens every year. Life is always waiting to bring something wonderful at the right time.

GO, YOU!

Draw a tricky situation or memory you've had to deal with.

You can stop to do triangle breathing anytime you want.

1. DEEP, SLOW BREATH IN

2. HOLD AND SMILE

3. DEEP, SLOW BREATH OUT

Add lots of detail to your picture.

Take your time to really notice every part of it, and color it carefully.

Keep going until your whole mind feels peaceful looking at the picture. You are **LETTING GO!**

Add some encouraging thoughts to remind yourself that you can cope with it now.

COLOR THIS IN

Fill these bubbles with any worries you want to get rid of.

Let them float up into the sky and pop,
taking your worries with them.

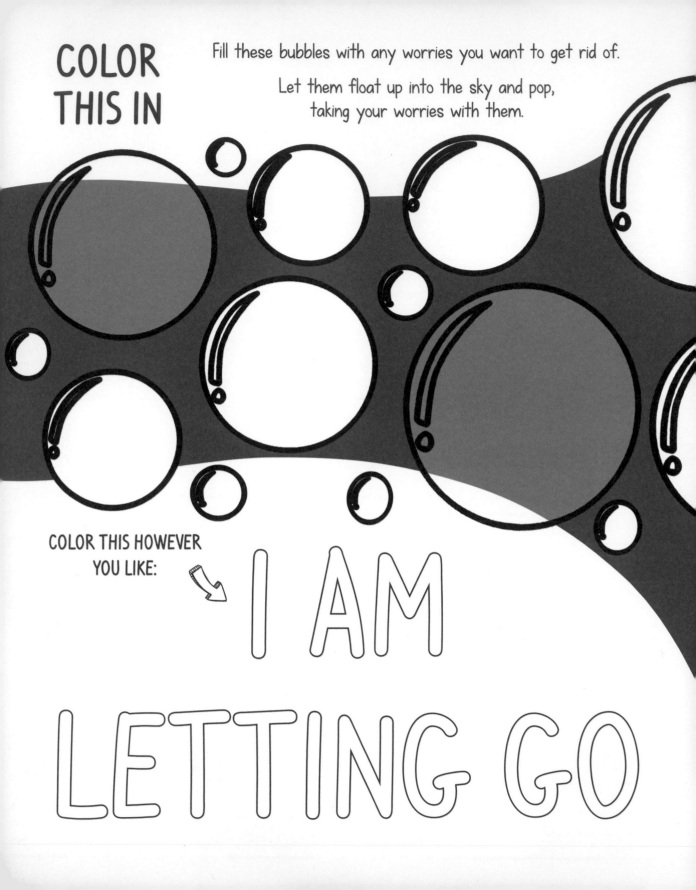

COLOR THIS HOWEVER
YOU LIKE:

I AM
LETTING GO

While you color this in, think of the things you need to let go of.

HEART OF GOLD

In Japan, the ancient art of KINTSUGI (金継ぎ) is used to mend broken pottery, using sap from trees and gold or silver powder.

We can feel like our heart is broken after upsetting things happen, but in time, we heal. This means we accept our loss, adjust, let go, and move forward.

We might still remember the hurt, but we choose not to be stuck in it or stay feeling broken.

Color this pot and decorate it however you want.

Make sure you color the cracks to show how unique and beautiful it is – just like you.

These pots that were once broken are considered unique and even more beautiful for having been broken.

Draw and color some cracks in this heart for the things that have happened in your history which make you unique and beautiful.

You can write what these things are on or around your heart, if you like.

POTS OF LOVE

Want to try practicing the Japanese art of KINTSUGI (金継ぎ)?

YOU WILL NEED:

- A helpful adult
- A small pot or old mug
- PVA glue

- Colorful pipe cleaners
- Gold or silver wrapping paper or pens

- Tissue paper
- Some gravel, clay, or flower arranging foam

Ask an adult to help you with this.

Cut strips of gold or silver paper and glue these onto your pot or mug to look like cracks, then paint on a coat of PVA glue all over the outside (not underneath the pot/mug). Or use a gold or silver pen to draw on the cracks.

Fill the pot (or mug) with gravel, clay, or foam. If you use gravel, you could mix it with some PVA glue so if it gets knocked over, it isn't too messy!

Make a flower and stem with the pipe cleaners and push it into the pot filling – make a hole first with a pencil if needed.

Make more flowers if you like.

You can use the picture as a template for folding and wrapping the pipe cleaners. Use more than one pipe cleaner for the stem if your flower is heavy. Use your imagination and go wild!

You could experiment with tissue paper for making flowers, too.

If you want to be a gardener, use soil and an apple, lemon, orange, or avocado seed instead – or any seed you have at home.

DESIGN YOUR POT HERE. Work out where you'd like the cracks to be and color them in.

Then make your pot of love as a gift for someone else or for yourself.

You can be a success wherever you are!

MEMORIES ARE MADE OF THIS

Fill this frame with wonderful memories of happy times, like a day trip, a special event, winning something, getting or giving a gift, vacations, family celebrations, or anything that you enjoyed.

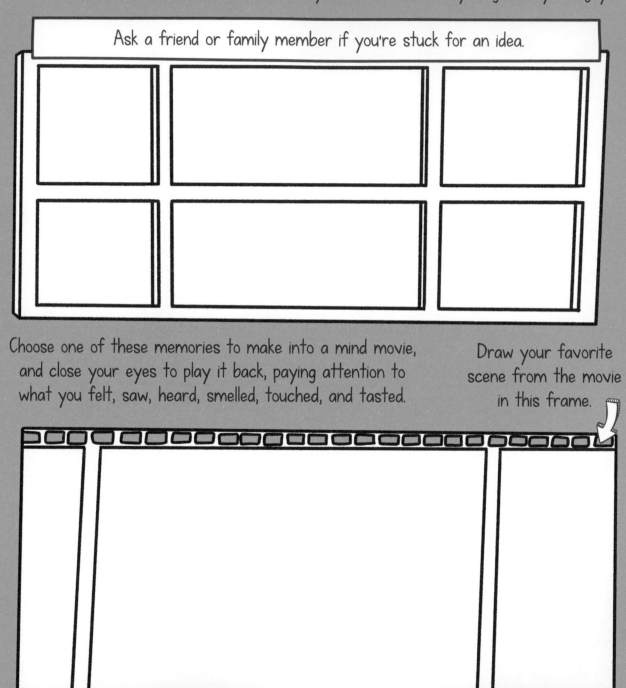

Ask a friend or family member if you're stuck for an idea.

Choose one of these memories to make into a mind movie, and close your eyes to play it back, paying attention to what you felt, saw, heard, smelled, touched, and tasted.

Draw your favorite scene from the movie in this frame.

NO REGRETS

It's OK to have regrets from time to time about things we did or didn't do, said or didn't say.

For every regret you have, there's something about you to be proud of.

Finish these sentences, put them through the forgiveness machine, and see what proud moments come out the other side.

Regrets are normal, but if they start to stay around for longer than you want, it's time to start **LETTING GO** of them.

I WISH I HADN'T
argued with my friend.

IF ONLY

IT WAS MY FAULT THAT

I'M SORRY THAT

I BLAME MYSELF FOR

I'M GLAD I
said sorry.

IT'S GREAT THAT

IT WAS HELPFUL WHEN I

I'M PROUD THAT

THANKS TO ME,

BE YOUR OWN HERO

A HERO HAS FOUR MAIN QUALITIES

HOPE — they believe that good things are possible.

ENERGY — they put effort into making good things happen.

RESILIENCE — they believe they can defeat obstacles and keep trying.

OPTIMISM — they believe in their own power to succeed.

Stand with your hands on your hips in front of a mirror.

Now smile and imagine you are your very own **HERO** who's going to support you and help you move forward. Think of other superheroes to inspire you, and then be creative.

Draw your own **HERO** reflection in the mirror and decorate your **FOUR HERO** qualities.

HOPE

OPTIMISM

You could design a costume if you like – or maybe just write **HERO** on your T-shirt.

The power is yours!

ENERGY

RESILIENCE

Make a mind movie where you use your **FOUR HERO** qualities to overcome something that is difficult right now.

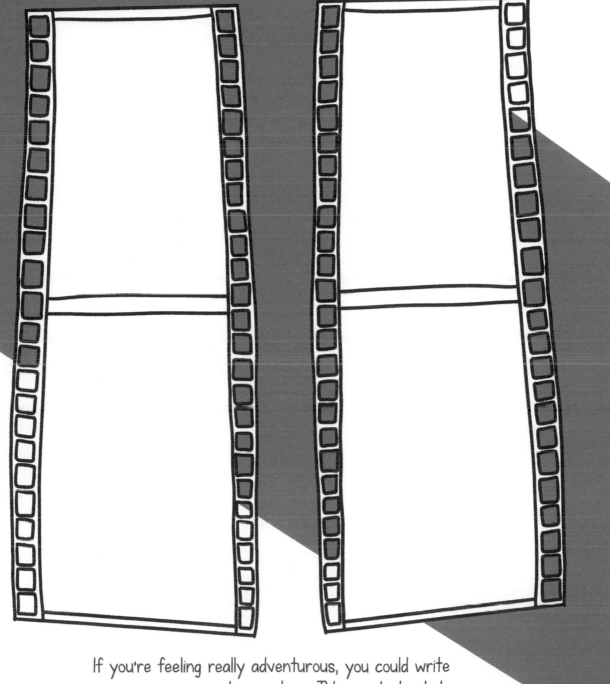

If you're feeling really adventurous, you could write a newspaper report or make a TV report about it.

DOODLE DASH

Dash the dog loves to doodle.

Help Dash fill this page with all kinds of random doodles.

GOING, GOING, GONE!

Let's get you ready to enjoy LETTING GO!

What thought, feeling, or idea do you need to let go of right now?

Imagine you've already made it happen. Make a set of photographs to show what you did.

1

2

3

4

Start at the end when the thought, feeling, or idea is gone, and work backward to show what you need to do to make it happen, and whose help you need.

START HERE!

How is life better now?

What can you do now that it's gone?

BUBBLE OF GRIEF

When you are grieving, you can feel trapped in a bubble and distant from other people or things around you.

Take your bubble high above the clouds, so you can see the bigger picture.

Do some 3:5 breathing for a few minutes.

Go where you can see a place below that is completely safe and comfortable.

A special, safe place where everything feels peaceful, calm, and safe.

Your safe place could be somewhere you've already seen or been to, heard about, read about, imagined, or dreamed about.

Notice everything about this safe place – colors, shapes, smells, sounds.

Slowly bring your bubble down and land there.

Sit in your bubble, just looking for a few minutes.

Now, step out of your bubble. Thank it for carrying you to this wonderful place, and let it go up into the sky for someone else to use.

YOU ARE SAFE HERE.

Draw your safe place in lots of detail, or find a picture from a magazine or a photo to stick on.

Spend five minutes staring at your picture, and make a mind movie of you being there and feeling like you are home again.

YOGA

Yoga is a great way to feel connected to the world.

TREE POSE

TREE POSE IS GREAT FOR FEELING BALANCED AND GETTING READY TO LET GO.

Stand up straight with your feet slightly apart. Take a deep breath and look ahead of you.

Breathe out.

Keep breathing smoothly and slowly bring up one foot and place it on the inside of your opposite leg. Reach your arms up and out like branches of a tree. Bring your hands together in front of your heart.

Lift your arms above your head like a growing tree! Hold the pose and imagine where you are growing – in a forest, a park, a town?

Say out loud – **I AM BALANCED.**

When you are ready, put your foot down and repeat the pose with the other leg.

CHILD'S POSE

RELAX YOUR BODY AND BE COMFORTABLE LETTING GO.

Kneel with your knees wide apart. Gently sit on your heels. Breathe in and sit up straight, stretching your back upward. Breathe out and lower your upper body so your heart and chest rest on your thighs.

Keep breathing smoothly.
Place your forehead on the floor. Stretch your arms along your sides, with your palms facing up. Hold for a minute or longer.

Say out loud – **I AM LETTING GO!**

When you are ready, gently turn your palms down, use your hands to walk your body back up, and sit on your heels.

MOUNTAIN POSE

BE STRONG AND STILL, LIKE A MOUNTAIN.

Stand tall with your feet slightly apart.

Sway very gently back and forth. Become still and strong from the inside out. Stand very still with your weight balanced evenly on your feet.

Put your arms straight beside your body and spread your fingers. Breathe deeply and hold this pose for as long as you are comfortable.

Say out loud – **I AM STRONG.**

MOUNTAINS TO CLIMB

Write along the outside of these mountains any things you are worried about doing or trying to get used to.

Color in your mountain range.

It might be the anniversary of something upsetting, coping with a special day without someone you'd want to have by your side, or something else you're not looking forward to.

When you've gotten through it, come back to this page and write along the paths what happened and how you managed it.

JUST PASSING THROUGH

Fill in these clouds with words or pictures of difficult things you've already let go of in your life.

See, you know how to do it!

NEW TEACHER

MOVING

DIVORCE

LOSS OF A PET

GO, YOU!

SAFETY WARNING – never look directly at the sun, even when wearing sunglasses.

Go outside and lie down somewhere safe and comfortable.

Do some 3:5 breathing to relax you. Watch the clouds in the sky passing overhead.

See how they change shape as you follow them.

LAND ART

Land art is a spectacular way to brighten up the day for anyone passing by.

Andy Goldsworthy is a famous artist who makes land art – look up his work for ideas if you like.

Be at one with nature. And make sure someone knows where you are!

In the yard, park, beach, or field, make some land art on the ground using only the natural things you find lying around.

Use pieces of wood, pods, seeds, shells, stones, leaves, or anything that you don't have to pick or break off.

Choose whether to make your picture really detailed, or use a simple shape from nature like a spiral, a heart, or whatever you like.

Leave your work in place for passersby to enjoy.

Draw your land art here. If you haven't been able to do this activity, just use your imagination and draw what you'd like to make from natural objects.

VOLCANO!

When your feelings rumble deep inside of you, it can be hard to know what to do.

Why not make a volcano in your kitchen that will get those feelings out in a safe and exciting way?

YOU WILL NEED:

- Clay or papier-mâché to make the volcano casing (optional)
- Clean container*
- Vinegar
- Mixing bowl
- Two drops of red food coloring (optional)
- Tablespoon of baking soda
- Tissues or paper towel
- Dish soap
- Rubber band

WARNING!
NEVER PUT A LID ON YOUR CONTAINER!

* e.g. a plastic beaker, jar, water bottle, dish soap bottle, shampoo bottle, or used can.

Ask an adult to help you with this activity.

If you want to make a clay or papier-mâché volcano casing, put the container on a flat surface and make a cone-shaped casing around it. Wait for it to dry if needed.

Mix the vinegar with red food coloring and a tablespoon of dish soap in a bowl.

Pour the mixture into the container.

Put the baking soda onto a tissue or a piece of paper towel and make a small sausage shape with it, holding it closed with a rubber band.

Make sure it is narrower than the opening of your volcano.

NOW DROP THIS INTO YOUR CONTAINER AND STAND BACK!

TIP   If you don't want to do lots of cleaning up afterward, it's best to do this outside, or on the draining board, or in the sink!

FLY AWAY HOME

This ladybug needs to fly home after a busy day. Fill her spots with feelings or memories you would like to let go of.

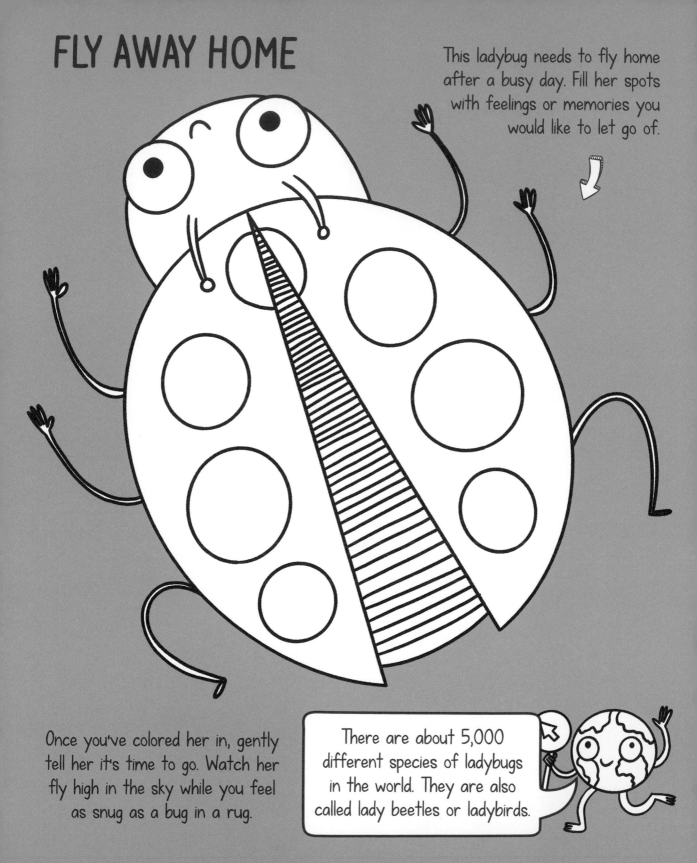

Once you've colored her in, gently tell her it's time to go. Watch her fly high in the sky while you feel as snug as a bug in a rug.

There are about 5,000 different species of ladybugs in the world. They are also called lady beetles or ladybirds.

Future you has been found and is smiling.

Make a found poster and then go and get your future – you deserve it!

FUTURE _____

FOUND!

NAME
_____

LET GO OF _____
~~~~~~~~~~~~~~~~~~~
~~~~~~~~~~~~~~~~~~~

NOW FEELS _____
~~~~~~~~~~~~~~~~~~~
~~~~~~~~~~~~~~~~~~~

STARFISH

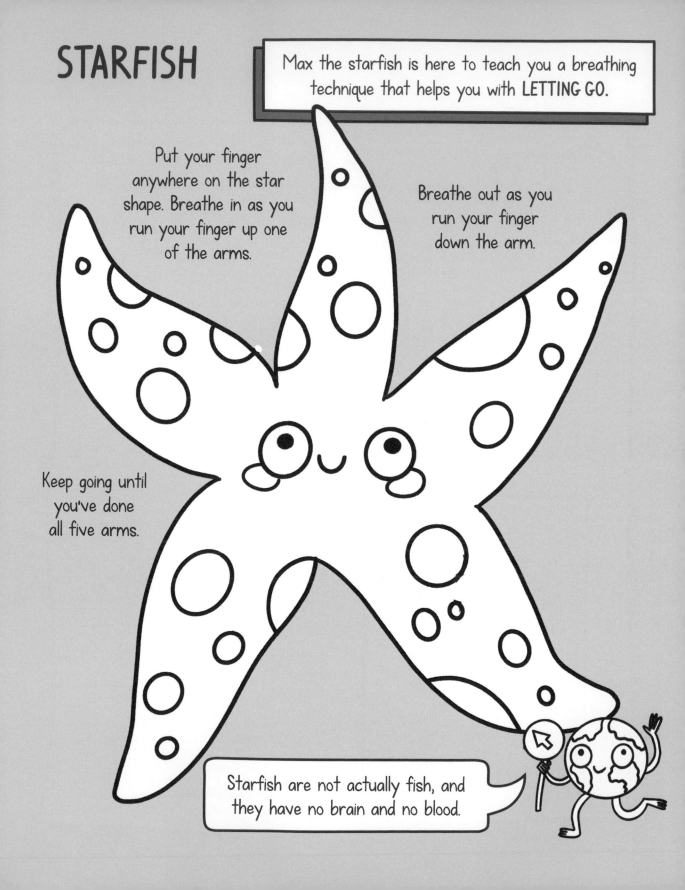

YOU make the world a better place and can make a big difference.

Walk along this beach full of stranded starfish.

Put them all back in the water.

You could draw them under the water or cover over where they already are with new water.

JUST ADD WATER

LETTING GO of the past can change your world for the better.

Add in all the creatures you want to see on your beach and in the ocean.

You could even make up imaginary ones.

Transform this dry, dusty desert into a beautiful beach, full of life and water.

Draw yourself enjoying the beach on a lovely day.

Draw in all the people you'd like to have there, enjoying it with you.

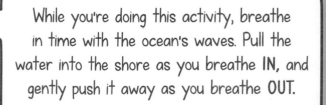

While you're doing this activity, breathe in time with the ocean's waves. Pull the water into the shore as you breathe IN, and gently push it away as you breathe OUT.

BUCKETS OF LOVE

Fill this bucket with things that make you feel special and loved.

DIG DEEP!

LIFE'S A BEACH

Every good sandcastle needs a flag.

Get creative designing your own flag to let everyone know this is your sandcastle. Include colors, patterns, or designs that really mean something to you.

Once you've finished, imagine the powerful tide coming in and covering over your sandcastle forever.

MEMORY STONES

Would you like to remember a person or a pet who was really special to you?

Maybe someone who helped you to achieve something or to feel happy. These stones are a good way to remember or mark special anniversaries or family events.

YOU WILL NEED:

- Stones
- Dish soap
- Warm water
- Paper towel
- Paint
- Permanent markers
- Printed words
- PVA glue and brush
- Scissors

Collect one or two large stones from your yard, or buy them from a nursery or craft shop.

Memory stones will look good in your room or placed carefully in a favorite spot outside.

You could even hide them on a walk you used to enjoy with the person or pet.

Wash and dry them completely on paper towel.

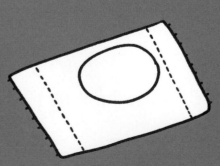

Decide what message you want to put on your stone.

PEACE

LOVE

It might be a name or some lovely words.

You can print your words, cut them out, and glue them on, or write them on the stones.

HOPE

TRUST

To make your stones last longer outside, paint PVA glue over the top.

If you want to throw your stone into the sea or a river, don't use PVA glue because it contains plastic.

MEMORY BOX

A memory box is a great way to celebrate a person or pet you loved.

You can use it to store special things that remind you of them and the relationship you have or had together.

YOU WILL NEED:

- Cardboard box with a lid
- Colored paper
- Paint
- Glue stick/tape
- Pens
- Scissors
- A picture of your loved one
- Magazines
- Decorations like buttons, ribbon, or stickers

Paint or cover your box with paper – perhaps in your special person's favorite color.

Put a photo on the box. Add any pictures and words you want to put on the box, too.

DECORATE THE BOX HOWEVER YOU LIKE.

Use your memory box to keep all your memories in one place,
and look through it when you want to feel close to them.

STUFFED TOY

CARDS FROM BIRTHDAYS AND OTHER SPECIAL OCCASIONS

MUSIC THAT WAS IMPORTANT TO YOU BOTH

OLD TICKETS

PHOTOS

THEIR FAVORITE PERFUME OR SMELL

ANYTHING THAT REMINDS YOU OF THEM

YOU COULD WRITE AND INCLUDE NOTES ABOUT:

Something you especially love about your relationship with them.

A memory that you find comforting.

A special time you shared together.

YOU COULD ALSO ADD MESSAGES LIKE:

"I love you because..."
"Thank you for..."
"What I miss most about you is..."

Something you enjoyed or laughed about together.

FRIENDLY WORDS

Try coming up with thoughtful and supportive responses in the boxes.

What might you say to a friend who is feeling upset about something they are finding it hard to let go of?

"I'll never get over it."

"Why am I so sad?"

"When will I feel OK again?"

"Why did that happen?"

NIGHT AND DAY

The sun shines all day and all night – even when you can't see it.

When the moon appears to scatter light across the dark night sky, it's actually the sun's light being reflected by the moon.

Color both sides of Flo, making one side of her in the dark and the other side in the light.

Day always follows night. The moon is our promise that a new day is on the way.

DREAM CATCHER

If you ever have a bad dream, don't worry – it's just how your brain makes sense of everything it sees, feels, learns, and wonders about during the day.

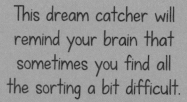

It's organizing all the bits of information, like when you sort recycling and trash or the laundry into different piles.

Your brain isn't trying to upset or frighten you. It thinks that because you're asleep, you won't notice the work it's doing.

This dream catcher will remind your brain that sometimes you find all the sorting a bit difficult.

Inside the big circle, write or draw the things that trouble or worry you at the moment, and trap them inside the lines going across, which you can color if you want.

Write what makes you feel safe in the boxes all around the outside – your strengths, favorite activities, things, or people you love and who love you.

The feathers help these lovely things breeze into your mind while you sleep.

Why not cut out your dream catcher and put it by your bed? Sweet dreams.

WISHING ON A STAR

Bedtime can remind us of things we find it hard to come to terms with.

Fill this star with all the things you wish for yourself, your loved ones, and the world.

Get them all out of your heart and mind and onto the paper.

Make the star look beautiful, or just fill it with your thoughts – or both!

Do this every night, if you want to, until you've gotten everything out and can start LETTING GO.

Now you can rest. Relax your breathing with soft breaths. Imagine one of these things coming true for you and take yourself into a lovely dream. Good night, wonderful you.

SETTLE DOWN

Taking time to prepare for bed will settle your brain so you can sleep well and wake up happy.

Breathe deeply and calmly for a few minutes while you're still sitting on your bed.

Do triangle breathing or 3:5 breathing by yourself or with someone else.

Get into bed and close your eyes for 10 seconds. Then open them again and count to 30. Repeat this three times.

Read a favorite book for about 10 minutes to help settle you.

Put the book down and then look at five things in your room that you love having near you – maybe a photo or a stuffed toy.

Tell yourself four pleasant things about the day you've had.

Say thank you in your mind or out loud for three people who helped you today – don't forget about yourself.

Think of two things you're looking forward to tomorrow.

Close your eyes and notice one thing you can feel, like your own breathing perhaps, the softness of your blanket, or anything else.

Draw yourself fast asleep, looking cozy, comfortable, and content.

TREASURE MAP

We can't always see what's waiting to bring us a smile, fun, happiness, and comfort.

LETTING GO gets you ready to find life's hidden treasures.

Make your own treasure map so you can remember that great things are everywhere, even when you can't see them.

Make a key if you like.

Give your map hidden treasures, like memories that make you happy, as well as some things to avoid, so you keep moving forward.

THE PAGE FOR GROWN-UPS

This activity book is perfect for parents, caregivers, teachers, learning mentors, therapists, social workers, and youth leaders who want to help children come to terms with upsetting life events so they can let go and move forward.

Life events sometimes knock children off course. Changing class or school, disappointments, friendship problems, moving, new family arrangements, sudden illness, or bereavement of beloved people or pets, all present difficult challenges. Children may experience confusion, hurt and angry feelings, anxiety, fearfulness, reduced trust and confidence in themselves or others, and feel lost or alone in the world. They can't always control or make choices about what happens next, potentially leaving them emotionally vulnerable, overwhelmed, and bewildered. Equally, you may not be able to prevent the uncertainties they'll have to face. You might notice an increase in their self-doubt, negative thoughts, stomachaches, headaches, or tiredness and avoidance of previously enjoyed people, places, or activities.

In loving, nurturing environments, children are resilient and might be able to work through problems without additional support. However, they might not have the knowledge or language skills to explain their distress, so may struggle to make sense of what is happening. This book helps children explore, express, and explain their grief and open up the conversation with you. The uplifting, reflective activities increase clarity, confidence, courage, and resilience, combat negativity and encourage a heathy understanding of their feelings and their world, enabling them to identify and process their emotions and, in time, let go.

Moving forward takes patience, support, and plenty of hugs. If your child's grief persists beyond three months or escalates, talk to their school, your doctor, a counselor, or one of the organizations listed below for support and guidance.

NATIONAL ALLIANCE ON MENTAL ILLNESS (NAMI)

Educate, advocate, listen, lead.

The NAMI HelpLine can be reached Monday through Friday, 10 am–6 pm, ET.

NAMI is the nation's largest grassroots mental health organization dedicated to building better lives for the millions of Americans affected by mental illness.

www.nami.org info@nami.org

Tel: 1-800-950-NAMI (6264)

GOODTHERAPY.ORG®

Helping people find therapists. Advocating for ethical therapy.

GoodTherapy.org offers a directory to help you in your search for a therapist. Using the directory, you can search by therapist location, specialization, gender, and age group treated. If you search by location, your results will include the therapists near you and will display their credentials, location, and the issues they treat.

Tel: 1-888-563-2112 ext. 1

www.goodtherapy.org

NATIONAL PARENT HELPLINE

Support and resources for parents worried about their children.

Tel: 1-855-4A PARENT (1-855-427-2736)

www.nationalparenthelpline.org